# Anno's Magical ABC
## an anamorphic alphabet
Mitsumasa Anno & Masaichiro Anno

THE BODLEY HEAD   *LONDON SYDNEY TORONTO*

British Library Cataloguing
in Publication Data
Anno, Mitsumasa
Anno's magical ABC
1. English language – Alphabet –
Juvenile literature
I. Title    II. Anno, Masaichiro
421´.1    PE1155
ISBN 0–370–30405–5

Printed and bound in Japan for
The Bodley Head Ltd,
9 Bow Street, London WC2E 7AL
*First published by Dowaya Co. Ltd, Tokyo, 1980*
*First published in Great Britain 1981*

# What is anamorphosis?

When you stand in front of a funny mirror in an amusement park the reflection of your face and body is distorted. In a concave mirror you look short and fat, in a cylindrical mirror you look tall and thin. The same is true of course of a reflected drawing or painting, and with a drawing or painting you can reverse the process. If you draw something warped and misshapen in a particular way and then look at it in a distorted mirror, its reflected image will look quite normal. This method of drawing is called anamorphosis and its purpose is solely to mystify and amuse.

The word anamorphosis seems first to have been used in the 17th century but the underlying principle of negative perspective was understood long before that by ancient Greek painters and sculptors who distorted the proportions of works designed to be exhibited in raised positions so that they would look normal when viewed from below.

Anamorphosis was once very popular in Europe and two fine examples of anamorphosis in painting are the portrait of Edward VI in the National Portrait Gallery in London, attributed to Cornelis Anthonisz in 1546, and the distorted skull of Holbein's Ambassadors (1533) in the National Gallery in London. In Japan too during the Edo period of 1600 – 1868 there was a type of anamorphic picture which was drawn to be reflected on the sheath of a sword.

In the middle of this book you will find an explanation of how you can do your own anamorphic painting or drawing.

# How to look at this book

Every new copy of *Anno's Magical ABC* has two sheets of mirror paper in a pocket inside the cover. Tape the paper round a drinking glass, an empty can, a bottle or a similar cylindrical object, and stand it in the middle of the page. Both the letter and the picture will spring into focus in the mirror. Keep the mirror paper clean by wiping it with a soft cloth.

If the original sheets of mirror paper have been used or lost here are a number of alternative suggestions:

* Take the label off a can of soup (or baked beans or anything) and use the can as a reflector.
* Stand a new roll of aluminium baking foil in the middle of the page. It must be new because once the foil is unrolled it creases and spoils the reflection.
* Buy new sheets of mirror paper at an art supply shop, or stainless steel or aluminium sheets at a hardware shop.

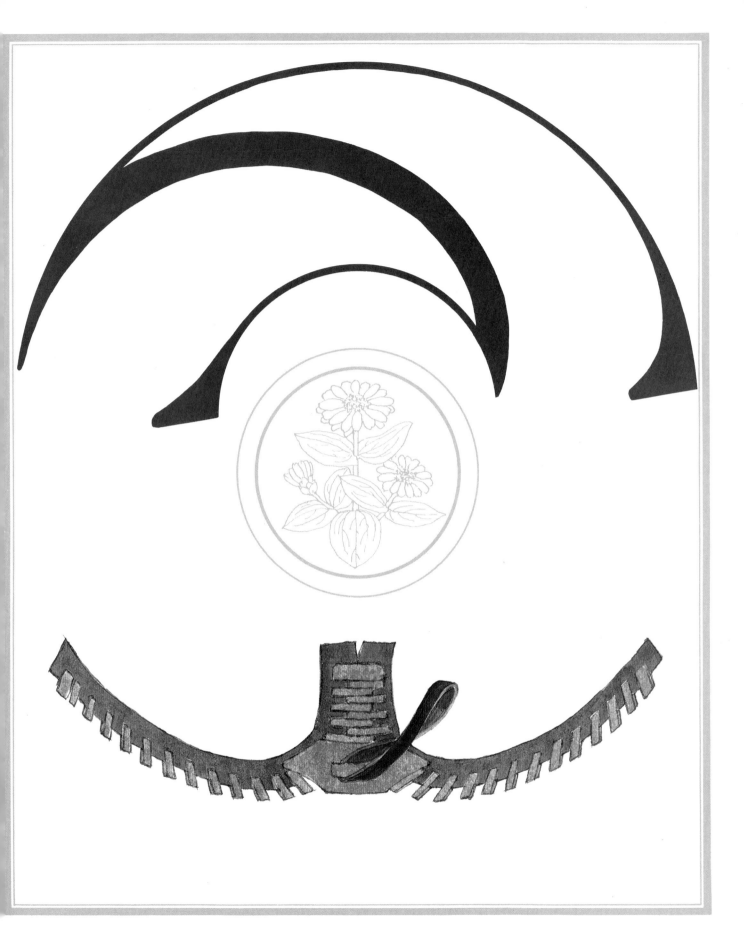

# Clues to Anno's spells

| | | | |
|---|---|---|---|
| **A** | Angel 天使 | ant, anteater アリ、アリクイ | apple リンゴ |
| **B** | Balalaika バラライカ | bee, bear ハチ、クマ | blackberry クロイチゴ |
| **C** | Cassette カセットテープ | camel ラクダ | clover クローバー |
| **D** | Doll 人形 | donkey ロバ | daisy デージー、ヒナギク |
| **E** | Elf, Egg 小びと、たまご | elephant ゾウ | elm ニレ |
| **F** | Faun フォーン牧神 (ローマ神話の半人半羊の林野牧畜の神) ギリシャ神話ではPan | fox キツネ | forget-me-not ワスレナグサ |
| **G** | Glider グライダー | goat ヤギ | gentian リンドウ |
| **H** | House 家 | horse ウマ | harebell イトシャジン |
| **I** | Ice cream アイスクリーム | iguana イグアナ | ivy ツタ |
| **J** | Jack ジャック | jaguar ジャガー | jasmine ジャスミン |
| **K** | King キング | kangaroo カンガルー | knapweed ヤグルマギクのなかま |
| **L** | Lamp ランプ | lion ライオン | lily ユリ |
| **M** | Mermaid 人魚 | mouse ネズミ | millet キビ |
| **N** | Nut-cracker くるみ割り | newt イモリ | nettle イラクサ |
| **O** | Ocarina オカリナ | ox ウシ | oak カシの木 |
| **P** | Pirate 海賊 | pig ブタ | poppy ポピー、ケシ |
| **Q** | Queen クィーン | quail ウズラ | quince マルメロ |
| **R** | Racquet ラケット | rabbit ウサギ | rose バラ |
| **S** | Ship 帆船 | squirrel リス | sun spurge トウダイグサ |
| **T** | Tricycle 三輪車 | tiger トラ | thistle アザミ |
| **U** | Umbrella かさ | unicorn ユニコーン、一角獣 | *urtica pilulifera* ( = roman nettle) イラクサのなかま |
| **V** | Violin バイオリン | vulture ハゲタカ | violet スミレ |
| **W** | Windmill 風車 | wolf オオカミ | walnut クルミの木 |
| **X** | Xylophone 木琴 | *xenus cinerius* ( = terek sandpiper) ソリハシシギ | *xanthium strumarium* ( = lesser burdock) オナモミ |
| **Y** | Yacht ヨット | yak ヤク | yew イチイ |
| **Z** | Zip ジッパー | zebra シマウマ | zinnia ヒャクニチソウ |

## About Mitsumasa Anno

Mitsumasa Anno was born in 1926 in Tsuwano, a small historic town in the western part of Japan. He graduated from Yamaguchi Teacher Training College and then worked as a primary school teacher before starting his career as an artist. Mr Anno now lives in Tokyo but he is a regular traveller to Europe and has visited the United States of America. A selection of his illustrations from 1968–1977 has been published as *The Unique World of Mitsumasa Anno* – and his many picture books for children include:

Anno's Alphabet
Anno's Animals
Anno's Counting Book
Anno's Journey
Anno's Italy
Anno's Medieval World
The King's Flower

# How to do an
# anamorphic drawing

Anamorphosis is not easy, but it is great fun. The reduced graphs on this page show you how it is done. On Graph A the letter K has been drawn in reverse and then transferred to Graph B, box by box. By now it is hard to see clearly what it is, but when reflected in a cylindrical mirror it comes back to its normal shape again.

You can draw an anamorphic picture in exactly the same way. First, trace out copies of the enlarged graphs from the opposite page, or make photocopies of them, so you can experiment as often as you like and still leave the clean graphs for the next person. Now draw your picture straightforwardly on your copy of Graph A and then transfer it, box by box, to your copy of Graph B. It is important to remember that letters and pictures have to be drawn in reverse because the reflected images will be seen from the other way up. Good luck.

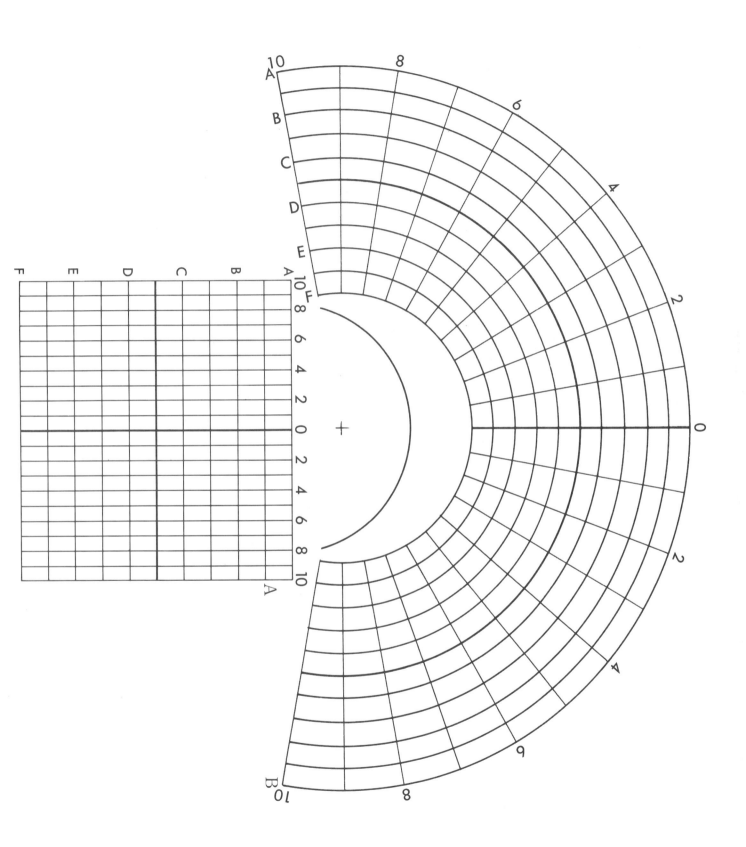

## About Masaichiro Anno

Masaichiro Anno was born in Tokyo in 1954. He graduated from the National Science and Engineering Division of Waseda University in Tokyo and is now working in advertising.

*Anno's Magical ABC* was his idea. He drew the letters and his father, Mitsumasa Anno, wrote the text and drew the pictures. The picture on the left is a mixture of the body of Mitsumasa and the face of Masaichiro. Reflected in your mirror this man should look slim but if you think he looks a bit fat it must be because he is wearing such heavy clothes.

# Clues to Anno's spells

| | | | |
|---|---|---|---|
| **A** | Angel 天使 | ant, anteater アリ、アリクイ | apple リンゴ |
| **B** | Balalaika バ ラ ラ イ カ | bee, bear ハチ、クマ | blackberry クロイチゴ |
| **C** | Cassette カセットテープ | camel ラクダ | clover クローバー |
| **D** | Doll 人形 | donkey ロバ | daisy デージー、ヒナギク |
| **E** | Elf, Egg 小びと、たまご | elephant ゾウ | elm ニレ |
| **F** | Faun フォーン牧神 (ローマ神話の半 人半羊の林野牧畜の神) ギリシャ神話 ではPan | fox キツネ | forget‑me‑not ワスレナグサ |
| **G** | Glider グライダー | goat ヤギ | gentian リンドウ |
| **H** | House 家 | horse ウマ | harebell イトシャジン |
| **I** | Ice cream アイスクリーム | iguana イグアナ | ivy ツタ |
| **J** | Jack ジャック | jaguar ジャガー | jasmine ジャスミン |
| **K** | King キング | kangaroo カンガルー | knapweed ヤグルマギクのなかま |
| **L** | Lamp ランプ | lion ライオン | lily ユリ |
| **M** | Mermaid 人魚 | mouse ネズミ | millet キビ |
| **N** | Nut‑cracker くるみ割り | newt イモリ | nettle イラクサ |
| **O** | Ocarina オカリナ | ox ウシ | oak カシの木 |
| **P** | Pirate 海賊 | pig ブタ | poppy ポピー、ケシ |
| **Q** | Queen クィーン | quail ウズラ | quince マルメロ |
| **R** | Racquet ラケット | rabbit ウサギ | rose バラ |
| **S** | Ship 帆船 | squirrel リス | sun spurge トウダイグサ |
| **T** | Tricycle 三輪車 | tiger トラ | thistle アザミ |
| **U** | Umbrella かさ | unicorn ユニコーン、一角獣 | *urtica pilulifera* (= roman nettle) イラクサのなかま |
| **V** | Violin バイオリン | vulture ハゲタカ | violet スミレ |
| **W** | Windmill 風車 | wolf オオカミ | walnut クルミの木 |
| **X** | Xylophone 木琴 | *xenus cinerius* (= terek sandpiper) ソリハシシギ | *xanthium strumarium* (= lesser burdock) オナモミ |
| **Y** | Yacht ヨット | yak ヤク | yew イチイ |
| **Z** | Zip ジッパー | zebra シマウマ | zinnia ヒャクニチソウ |

# What is anamorphosis?

When you stand in front of a funny mirror in an amusement park the reflection of your face and body is distorted. In a concave mirror you look short and fat, in a cylindrical mirror you look tall and thin. The same is true of course of a reflected drawing or painting, and with a drawing or painting you can reverse the process. If you draw something warped and misshapen in a particular way and then look at it in a distorted mirror, its reflected image will look quite normal. This method of drawing is called anamorphosis and its purpose is solely to mystify and amuse.

The word anamorphosis seems first to have been used in the 17th century but the underlying principle of negative perspective was understood long before that by ancient Greek painters and sculptors who distorted the proportions of works designed to be exhibited in raised positions so that they would look normal when viewed from below.

Anamorphosis was once very popular in Europe and two fine examples of anamorphosis in painting are the portrait of Edward VI in the National Portrait Gallery in London, attributed to Cornelis Anthonisz in 1546, and the distorted skull of Holbein's Ambassadors (1533) in the National Gallery in London. In Japan too during the Edo period of 1600 – 1868 there was a type of anamorphic picture which was drawn to be reflected on the sheath of a sword.

In the middle of this book you will find an explanation of how you can do your own anamorphic painting or drawing.

# How to look at this book

Every new copy of *Anno's Magical ABC* has two sheets of mirror paper in a pocket inside the cover. Tape the paper round a drinking glass, an empty can, a bottle or a similar cylindrical object, and stand it in the middle of the page. Both the letter and the picture will spring into focus in the mirror. Keep the mirror paper clean by wiping it with a soft cloth.

If the original sheets of mirror paper have been used or lost here are a number of alternative suggestions:
* Take the label off a can of soup (or baked beans or anything) and use the can as a reflector.
* Stand a new roll of aluminium baking foil in the middle of the page. It must be new because once the foil is unrolled it creases and spoils the reflection.
* Buy new sheets of mirror paper at an art supply shop, or stainless steel or aluminium sheets at a hardware shop.

British Library Cataloguing
in Publication Data
Anno, Mitsumasa
Anno's magical ABC
1. English language – Alphabet –
Juvenile literature
I. Title    II. Anno, Masaichiro
421´.1    PE1155
ISBN 0–370–30405–5

Printed and bound in Japan for
The Bodley Head Ltd,
9 Bow Street, London WC2E 7AL
*First published by Dowaya Co. Ltd, Tokyo, 1980*
*First published in Great Britain 1981*

# Anno's Magical A B C
## an anamorphic alphabet
### Mitsumasa Anno & Masaichiro Anno

THE BODLEY HEAD  *LONDON SYDNEY TORONTO*